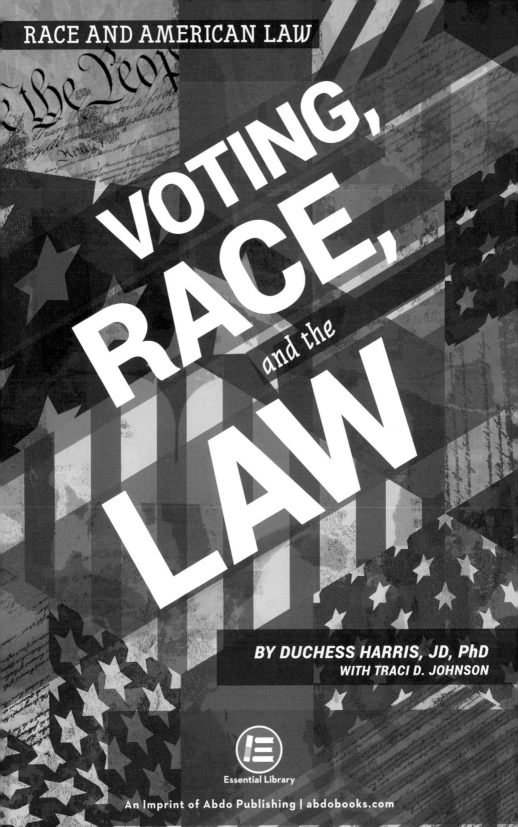

RACE AND AMERICAN LAW

VOTING, RACE, and the LAW

BY DUCHESS HARRIS, JD, PhD

WITH TRACI D. JOHNSON

Essential Library

An Imprint of Abdo Publishing | abdobooks.com

Published by Abdo Publishing, a division of ABDO, PO Box 398166, Minneapolis, Minnesota 55439. Copyright © 2020 by Abdo Consulting Group, Inc. International copyrights reserved in all countries. No part of this book may be reproduced in any form without written permission from the publisher. Essential Library™ is a trademark and logo of Abdo Publishing.

Printed in the United States of America, North Mankato, Minnesota.
082019
012020

Interior Photos: Jake Schoellkopf/AP Images, 5; Scott Sonner/AP Images, 9; David Howells/Corbis Historical/Getty Images, 10; iStockphoto, 13; North Wind Picture Archives, 14; Jacquelyn Martin/ AP Images, 16; Everett Collection/Newscom, 21, 22; Pictorial Press Ltd/Alamy, 25; Everett Historical/ Shutterstock Images, 28, 31; AP Images, 32, 45, 46, 49; Historical/Corbis Historical/Getty Images, 35; H.S. Photos/Alamy, 37; Atlanta Journal-Constitution/AP Images, 40; Joseph Sohm/Shutterstock Images, 53; RosalreneBetancourt 7/Alamy, 57; Pable Martinez Monsivais/AP Images, 58; Evan Vucci/ AP Images, 60; Rob Crandall/Shutterstock Images, 63; Mark Ralston/AFP/Getty Images, 67; John Marshall Mantel/Rapport Press/Newscom, 68; Rogelio V. Solis/AP Images, 70; Light Field Studios/ iStockphoto, 74; Gino Santa Maria/Shutterstock Images, 76; Sundry Photography/Shutterstock Images, 79; John Minchillo/AP Images, 83; Marc Levy/AP Images, 87; Mark Wallheiser/UPI/Newscom, 89; Wilfredo Lee/AP Images, 94–95; Carlos Giusti/AP Images, 97

Editor: Alyssa Krekelberg
Series Designer: Becky Daum

LIBRARY OF CONGRESS CONTROL NUMBER: 2019941947
PUBLISHER'S CATALOGING-IN-PUBLICATION DATA

Names: Harris, Duchess, author. | Johnson, Traci D., author.
Title: Voting, race, and the law / by Duchess Harris and Traci D. Johnson
Description: Minneapolis, Minnesota : Abdo Publishing, 2020 | Series: Race and American law | Includes online resources and index.
Identifiers: ISBN 9781532190292 (lib. bdg.) | ISBN 9781532176142 (ebook)
Subjects: LCSH: Race relations--Juvenile literature. | Race discrimination--Law and legislation—Juvenile literature. | Voting--United States--Juvenile literature. | Voting rights-- Juvenile literature.
Classification: DDC 305.89--dc23

CONTENTS

CHAPTER ONE

NATIVE AMERICANS AND VOTING RIGHTS

I n 2018, the United States had its midterm elections. Midterm elections happen between presidential races. During these elections, every member of the House of Representatives is up for reelection. Some senators are up for reelection as well. These elections are important because they decide who controls the House in Congress.

North Dakota was home to one of the most closely watched Senate races in the country. President Donald Trump had won the state by more than 30 points in 2016 when he ran for president.[1] North Dakota voters tended to vote Republican—Trump's party. The president had also endorsed Republican Kevin Cramer, who served in the House of Representatives, in Cramer's run for the Senate seat.

Voting is an important right for people in the United States.

Running against Cramer was Democrat incumbent Heidi Heitkamp. It was highly likely that she would lose her seat. But one of Heitkamp's strengths was her popularity with Native American voters, such as people from the Spirit Lake Sioux Tribe. At that time, Native Americans were approximately 5.5 percent of the state's population.[2] In fact, the state had one of the highest percentages of Native American potential voters in the United States. However, a few weeks before the election, the US Supreme Court allowed a new North Dakota voter ID law to go into effect—one that could hinder Native Americans from voting.

THE NORTH DAKOTA VOTER ID LAW

The North Dakota law required voters to show identification that included their legal name, date of birth, and residential street address. The law also stated that PO boxes would no longer be considered acceptable addresses. However, thousands of Native Americans don't have street addresses, in part due to a high homelessness rate. Also, the federal reservations where many Native Americans live often don't have street addresses.

The ID law was passed in 2017. Voting rights advocates immediately took the state to court to prevent its enforcement. They argued the law was unfair since many tribal IDs lack a residential address. The law *did* allow the use of documents such as utility bills to prove the address, but many Native Americans in North Dakota didn't have access to those either.

Between 2013 and 2015, North Dakota's legislature had ended the right to vote without ID. It also ended the right to vote if an election volunteer could prove the voter's identity. Since

Living on Reservations: The Difficulties of Voting

Voting can be very hard for people who live on reservations. In many rural areas, polling places are far apart, and it may take several hours to get to a polling site. Many Native Americans don't own cars and may have no way to get to the polling place.

In addition, many Native Americans don't have mailboxes. They may not have mailboxes because reservations are often located in extremely rural areas. Others prefer to have a PO box because of concerns about theft and vandalism. Native Americans also may not have easy access to a post office. This makes mailing ballots difficult. Additionally, some states consider it a crime to mail someone else's ballot. This means that neighbors can't drop off each other's ballots at the post office.

Native North Dakotans helped Heitkamp win a close race in 2012, voting rights activists believed the new laws were created to lower Native voter turnout in future elections. Activists pointed to numbers that showed a 12-point decrease in voter turnout between 2012 and 2014 after the new laws had gone into effect.[5] The decrease was seen in Rolette County, which has a majority Native American population.

Native American Voting Rights Act of 2018

The Native American Voting Rights Act was introduced in October 2018. Senator Tom Udall of New Mexico explained the act by saying that states were creating too many barriers for Native American voters. He was especially concerned about the effect of voter ID laws and fewer polling places. The bill proposes increasing access to voter registration sites and polling locations and permitting tribal ID cards for voting purposes. It would also require states to get permission from the Department of Justice before creating new requirements that might restrict voter turnout.

Speaking of the new law, Standing Rock Sioux Tribe chairperson Mike Faith said, "Why is it getting harder and harder for Native Americans to vote? This law clearly discriminates against Native Americans in North Dakota."[6]

THE NEW BATTLE

Voter ID laws are part of the new battlefront in voting rights. Some states have strict photo ID rules for voting, allowing only government-issued IDs. Other states allow voters to show multiple forms of ID to cast a ballot. The North Dakota law shows there are two opposing

Vinton Hawley of Nevada's Pyramid Lake Paiute Tribe, *left*, was one tribal chairperson who filed a lawsuit against Nevada's secretary of state. The lawsuit said people in two Native tribes experienced voter discrimination from the state.

sides on this issue. On one side are Democrats and civil rights advocates. They want voting to be as easy as possible. On the other side are Republicans and groups concerned about voter fraud. They want stricter voting laws to make sure no one can cheat at the voting booth by voting with a fake identity, voting more than once, selling a vote, or voting when ineligible. But neither side agrees on the reason for or the impact of these ID laws.

One of the organizations involved in the fight over voting rights is the American Civil Liberties Union (ACLU). The ACLU focuses on protecting the individual rights and liberties listed in the US Constitution. Speaking of the North Dakota law, the ACLU said, "This may seem like an [innocent] requirement, but in practice, it's likely to [block the vote of] thousands of Native Americans."[7]

North Dakota Republicans disagreed. Jim Silrum, North Dakota's deputy secretary of state, said the law was written after citizens and state representatives raised concerns about the possibility of voter fraud.

THE VERDICT

On election night 2018, Heitkamp lost by 11 points.[8] Republicans won the Senate seat, but Native American activists also won. Despite the ID law, Native turnout for the midterm elections was very high. In fact, in some Native areas, turnout was higher than it had been for the 2008 presidential election.

Many people try to encourage US citizens to vote.

The battle over voter ID wouldn't end with the North Dakota midterm election. In 2018, 35 states had laws requiring voters to show identification in order to vote. Those who defend ID laws and those who dislike them aren't any closer to agreeing on whether they hurt or help voters.

The struggle for voting rights in the United States is a long one. It stretches back to the birth of the country and reaches through the era of slavery, the Civil War (1861–1865), and Reconstruction (1865–1877). Voting rights struggles continued through the 1900s and affected many people, including African Americans, Latinos, and Asian Americans. The fight for voting rights still matters today. The debate over who should vote affected both the 2016 presidential election and the 2018 midterm elections. The battle for voting rights in the United States is not over.

DISCUSSION STARTERS

- Should it be necessary for voters to show identification to vote? Explain your opinion.

- Do you think it's fair that some US citizens face barriers when trying to vote? Explain your answer.

- How far should states go to prevent fraudulent voting? If some voters are inconvenienced or unable to vote because of anti-fraud efforts, is that OK? Explain your reasoning.

CHAPTER TWO

THE LONG PATH TO THE BLACK MAN'S VOTE

To English settlers in 1607, colonial Virginia was an unknown wilderness and their new home. Once they arrived safely, the settlers' concerns turned to government. They needed to choose a leader. Only 18 days after they landed, they cast their first votes. There were 105 men in the group.[1] But they all wouldn't have a say in deciding who would lead. Just seven of them had been secretly selected in England to serve as the group's governing council. Only six of those men were considered eligible to serve as council president.[2]

Thirteen years later, 102 English settlers sailing to Virginia arrived instead on the rocky shores of Massachusetts.[3] They were the passengers on the *Mayflower*. Since the ship didn't land in Virginia, the settlers threw out their original agreement and

It has been a long, difficult journey for black men to get the right to vote.

It took the *Mayflower* approximately two months to cross the Atlantic Ocean.

created a new set of laws to govern themselves. They called their laws the Mayflower Compact. Only the adult males in the group were allowed to vote and sign the agreement. The group was made up of 41 men and included two indentured servants.[4]

As these stories show, the earliest voters in what would become the United States were all white males. Latinos and Asian Americans weren't represented among the very earliest settlers. Additionally, women, Native Americans, and African Americans couldn't vote in the English colonies. From the very beginning of American history, the right to vote was exclusive.

THE THREE-FIFTHS COMPROMISE

In 1787, the United States was a brand-new nation. Its founders had to decide how the nation should be governed, but they were stuck on how to count the enslaved population. This count of enslaved people would help decide how many representatives each state would have in the new Congress. Many of the founders struggled with the issue of slavery, and some had considered freeing enslaved people. But instead of using the Constitution to move the country away from slavery, the founders agreed to a compromise. Their three-fifths compromise allowed states to count an enslaved individual as three-fifths of a person. This rule increased the states' population counts and thus the number of representatives they sent to Congress.

The Constitution became the law of the land by 1789. But the issue of black voting rights wasn't considered in the original document. The United States as a whole wouldn't deal with black voting rights until after the Civil War. However, for a period following the Constitution's ratification, several states allowed free blacks to vote. These included New Jersey, where both women and free blacks could vote. According to *Smithsonian* magazine, New Jersey law said voters had to be "free inhabitants of [the] State."[5] They also had to be a certain age, have a certain amount of money, and have resided in the state for more than half a year. In most states, voting rights for free blacks only

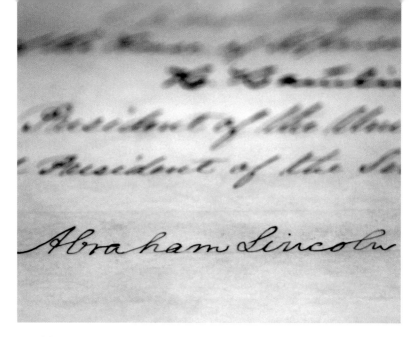

President Abraham Lincoln was assassinated before the Thirteenth Amendment was ratified by the states. However, months before his death, he signed the proposed amendment passed by Congress.

lasted for a brief period of time. By 1807, the New Jersey law had changed so that only adult white male taxpayers could vote.

THE FIRST TASTE OF FREEDOM: THIRTEENTH, FOURTEENTH, AND FIFTEENTH AMENDMENTS

Enslaved African Americans gained their freedom in 1865 when the Thirteenth Amendment to the Constitution outlawed slavery. But it would take three more years for black people to be recognized as US citizens.

The Fourteenth Amendment (1868) gave full rights to people born in the United States and to immigrants who received US citizenship. The law was written to make sure formerly enslaved people would have equal protection under the laws. But neither of these amendments granted African Americans the right to vote.

African American men faced many barriers to receive their voting rights. In 1865, a group of black people from Tennessee argued their cause to a group of pro-Union whites. They said, "If we are called on to do military duty against the rebel armies in the field, why should we be denied the privilege of voting against rebel citizens at the ballot-box?"[6] The famous freedom fighter Frederick Douglass also spoke out for black voting rights. He wrote, "It is no less a crime against the manhood of a man, to

The Split between Women and Black Activists

In the 1800s, the fight for the vote was a prize that united blacks and women activists, who were also called suffragists. But the battle to pass the Fifteenth Amendment, which would give black men the right to vote, broke up this alliance. It also broke up the friendship of two famous Americans, Frederick Douglass and Elizabeth Cady Stanton. Stanton had been an antislavery activist but opposed the passage of the Fifteenth Amendment because it didn't include women. Stanton said, "Shall American statesmen . . . so amend their constitutions as to make their wives and mothers the political inferiors of unlettered and unwashed ditch-diggers, bootblacks, butchers and barbers, fresh from the slave plantations of the South?"[7]

Douglass, who supported the amendment, said, "When women, because they are women, are hunted down through the cities of New York and New Orleans; when they are dragged from their houses and hung from lampposts; when their children are torn from their arms and their brains dashed out upon the pavement; when they are objects of insult and rage at every turn; when they are in danger of having their homes burnt down . . . then they will have an urgency to obtain the ballot equal to our own."[8]

Western Opposition to the Fifteenth Amendment

Opposition to the Fifteenth Amendment giving black men the right to vote wasn't confined to the South. Oregon and California also voted against it. In the 1800s, Oregon had a history of antiblack laws. Oregon law refused residence for black settlers and even allowed blacks to be whipped if they didn't leave. In California, some lawmakers believed Chinese immigrants, Mexicans, and blacks were inferior to whites and were uninterested in supporting a law that extended protections to everyone. Since many Chinese immigrants and people of Chinese ancestry lived in California, they were the focus of California's racial violence. In fact, local anti-immigrant groups such as the Ku Klux Klan terrorized Chinese residents and churches.

declare that he shall not share in the making and directing of the government under which he lives, than to say that he shall not acquire property and education."[9] But to gain voting rights, African Americans would need powerful allies among Northern Republicans. Republicans were the party in power after the Civil War. Many of them believed that granting all blacks the ability to vote would give the party more power in the North and especially the South. However, granting blacks the right to vote wasn't popular. Several Northern states put black voting rights to a vote in the 1860s, and those efforts were all defeated. Opponents of a federal law to support black voting rights also feared giving up state control over voting. The states were used to determining their own electoral requirements regarding race and didn't want to give that power to the federal government.

Despite this resistance, Congress passed the Fifteenth Amendment to the Constitution in 1869. One year later, the required amount of states had ratified the amendment, and it became law. The law prevents the US government or states from denying people the right to vote because of their race, color, or former status as a slave— but not their sex. After the amendment was ratified, African American men gained the right to vote.

Women's Voting Rights

The women's voting rights movement was born in 1848. That was the year of the first Women's Rights Convention. Convention members agreed to 11 resolutions on women's rights. One resolution stated, "*Resolved*, That it is the duty of the women of this country to secure to themselves their sacred right to the elective franchise [the vote]."[10]

But it would take decades of protesting and organizing before the movement succeeded. Congress passed the Nineteenth Amendment granting women the right to vote in 1919. The amendment was ratified by enough states to become law by 1920.

DISCUSSION STARTERS

- Should states or the federal government determine voting rights? Why?

- How do stereotypes play a role in stripping people of their rights as US citizens?

CHAPTER THREE

RECONSTRUCTION AND BLACK VOTING POWER

I n the early 1860s, many black people in the United States were still enslaved. Those who were free didn't have a constitutional right to vote or any guarantee of US citizenship. During Reconstruction, people who had been enslaved could vote in elections. Suddenly, Southern whites had to share power with the black people they had fought to keep enslaved. African Americans were elected to many powerful positions, such as representatives, senators, and governors.

BLACK POLITICIANS

The story of Robert Smalls was possible only because of Reconstruction. In 1862, Smalls was enslaved on a Confederate steamship, the *Planter*. In May of that year, the ship was docked in the harbor at Charleston, South Carolina. Smalls decided to

Robert Smalls served as a South Carolina congressperson for five terms.

steal the ship while the white officers were on shore. During the escape, Smalls guided the ship past every possible danger. He was even able to stop the ship and pick up his enslaved wife and children from the nearby West Atlantic Wharf without being captured. He flashed the correct navy signals to avoid being detected by the Confederates at Fort Johnson and Fort Sumter. Then he managed to surrender the ship to the Union navy without being fired upon. Smalls brought himself and all the slaves on board to freedom.

 Some black politicians—such as Blanche Bruce, Frederick Douglass, and Hiram Revels—are celebrated in artwork.

His place in history would have ended with the dramatic story of his escape if not for Reconstruction. In 1874, Smalls became a South Carolina congressman. Smalls would continue to serve in government positions until 1913.

Smalls wasn't the only formerly enslaved person to become an elected official from a former slave state. All over the South, black men were elected into office during Reconstruction. In fact, at one point African American men held the majority of seats in the South Carolina statehouse. Historian and author Eric Foner estimated that by 1877, around 2,000 black men held various official government positions in the United States.[1]

Senator Blanche Kelso Bruce

Blanche Kelso Bruce was the first African American elected to a full term in the Senate. Bruce had been born into slavery in Virginia. Although it was illegal to teach slaves to read, he was allowed to be educated alongside his white half-brother.

After the Civil War, Bruce moved to Mississippi, where he became a plantation owner and Republican politician. Bruce was elected to the Senate in 1874. As a senator, he fought for the rights of black veterans. Bruce left the Senate in 1881 when the Democrats took control of Mississippi.

RADICAL RECONSTRUCTION

The gains made by black officials were possible because of Radical Reconstruction. Radical Reconstruction was the second try at restructuring state governments in the South after the

Civil War. The first attempt at Reconstruction was watered down by President Andrew Johnson, who took office after President Abraham Lincoln was assassinated in 1865. Johnson was a Southerner who believed strongly in states' rights and held racist views. He gave the Confederate states the right to rebuild their governments as they saw fit. The Southern states reacted by passing Black Codes that restricted the rights of former slaves. They even sent Confederate military officials to represent the South in Congress. As a result, Northern Republican voters and politicians decided to restrain the Southern states by passing the Reconstruction Acts of 1867.

The Reconstruction Acts of 1867 divided the South into five military districts. Each of these states was forced to accept the Fourteenth Amendment. They were also forced to rewrite their state constitutions with the approval of their African American voters. The acts also limited the rights of some former Confederates to run for office and vote.

Black Codes

Immediately after the Civil War, the Southern states passed laws known as Black Codes. The laws were written to limit the rights of newly freed blacks. Under these codes, blacks weren't allowed to testify against whites in court, serve on juries, or vote. Blacks were also unable to carry guns and couldn't look for new jobs without a white employer's permission. These laws were overturned during Reconstruction. But the Southern states would seek to enforce them again once white Democrats returned to power in the late 1800s. These antiblack laws were known as Jim Crow laws.

These changes brought white and black Republicans to political power across the South. Additionally, millions of African Americans were able to vote for the first time. This was the country's first real attempt at interracial democracy, and many white Southerners hated it. They also disliked the Northerners who came to rebuild the South after the war. These Northern missionaries, teachers, soldiers, and Republican politicians were called *carpetbaggers*. White Southerners viewed carpetbaggers as greedy people who took advantage of a weak South.

Many white Southerners also falsely believed that the new black politicians were illiterate and unfit to serve in government. Despite the opposition, Republicans were successful in rebuilding roads, bridges, schools, and hospitals across the South. Antiblack white Southern Democrats began using threats and violence to regain power.

When they tried to practice their civil rights, black men were often threatened with violence by racist white Southerners.

WHITE VIOLENCE

The deadliest Reconstruction violence against blacks was known as the Opelousas Massacre. The massacre took place in Louisiana two months before the 1868 presidential election and was seen as an effort to keep blacks from voting Republican.

The 1866 New Orleans Massacre

In July 1866, a group of black men marched to the Republican-led state constitutional convention in New Orleans, Louisiana. A new constitution was being written to include the right to vote for black men. At the same time, a white mob led by the mayor was preparing to stop them. The mayor directed police to shoot the marchers. Marchers were also stabbed, beaten, and clubbed to death. When the violence ended, 50 people, mostly black, were dead, and as many as 200 had been injured.[2] The New Orleans Massacre—along with similar violence in Memphis, Tennessee—outraged Northern whites and was used to support the call for black civil rights in the South.

That summer, blacks had helped elect a Republican governor in Louisiana. This upset white Democrats, who began killing black families in and around Opelousas, Louisiana, as punishment for Republican victories. When a white Republican named Emerson Bentley wrote about this violence in his newspaper, a white Democratic mob responded by beating him. A small number of black residents armed themselves to defend Bentley and were greatly outnumbered by a white mob composed of thousands of people. The racial violence continued for weeks. Armed white men went from house to house searching for black people to arrest or kill. Some blacks were able to save themselves by swearing loyalty to the Democratic party. After two weeks, hundreds of black residents had been killed in their homes or shot in public. The violence was effective. There wasn't a single Republican vote cast in the area during the presidential election that fall.

THE END OF RECONSTRUCTION

As the 1870s progressed, the Reconstruction-era governments of the South began to fail. In 1883, black Americans lost the protections of the Civil Rights Act of 1875 when the Supreme Court ruled the act unconstitutional. The act forbade racial

The Rise of the Ku Klux Klan

In Tennessee, a formerly enslaved man reported being tied to a log and whipped after voting Republican. In Mississippi, a man's throat was slit and his intestines cut out in front of his wife. The Ku Klux Klan was responsible for both of these attacks.

The Klan began in 1865 as a social group for ex-Confederate soldiers. In the beginning, they adopted secret traditions and costumed ceremonies. During their gatherings, Klansmen became known for wearing white sheets to give the impression that ghosts of dead Confederate soldiers were riding through the countryside. The Klan also went night riding like the old slave patrols that had pursued runaway slaves.

The group soon became a dangerous terrorist organization. The Klan killed thousands of people and weakened the power of Republicans and blacks in the South. They were considered such a deadly threat that Congress passed the Ku Klux Klan Act in 1871. The law allowed the federal government to take action against the Klan using any tool necessary—including the military.

discrimination in hotels, trains, and other public places. The Supreme Court overturned the act because the majority of justices felt that Congress could only regulate states, not private individuals.

In 1877, Republican president Rutherford B. Hayes agreed to end further national efforts to enforce the rights of blacks. The last black politician elected during Reconstruction left Congress in 1901. Black politicians from the South wouldn't return to Congress until the 1970s. The first era of black political power and voting rights in the South was over. It would take the Voting Rights Act of 1965 to bring black politicians back into office in large numbers.

DISCUSSION STARTERS

- Why did racial violence happen so frequently during Reconstruction? Is there still the possibility for this type of violence today?

- How do you think it would feel to get the right to vote after spending years being prohibited from doing so?

- Do you think the US government did enough to stop white Southerners from oppressing black people? Explain your answer.

CHAPTER FOUR

VOTING RIGHTS ROLLBACK

The years after Reconstruction were difficult ones for people of color in the United States. In the western part of the country, it was a time of anti-immigrant hatred toward Chinese people living in the United States. That hatred led to laws prohibiting citizenship and voting rights for Chinese people. In the South, law after law was passed to turn the clock back on black rights. As a result, black voting rights were being brutally stamped out. Conditions wouldn't improve much for either of these groups for almost a century.

THE EXPULSION OF THE CHINESE

One winter night in 1886, a small group of whites pretending to be health inspectors entered Chinatown in Seattle, Washington. They forced their way into the homes of many Chinese residents.

Some Chinese immigrants were victims of violence from white people in the 1800s.

Chinatowns developed in cities such as San Francisco, California, *pictured*; Los Angeles, California; and Chicago, Illinois.

The whites dragged more than 300 Chinese people out of their beds and put them out on the street with their belongings.[1] Then they marched the Chinese to a steamship to force them out of the city. The next day, approximately 200 Chinese residents left the city on the ship. But 100 were left under the protection of the Seattle Home Guards.

As the guards attempted to escort the remaining Chinese to safety, they were met by an angry crowd of thousands of people. The crowd attacked the Home Guards, and shots were fired. Five people were injured, and one man later died. The violence didn't end until President Grover Cleveland sent in federal troops.

Because of this anti-Chinese violence, only a small number of Chinese chose to remain in Seattle after the expulsion. However, Seattle wasn't the only city that lashed out at its Chinese residents. During the mid-1880s, similar incidents occurred in Tacoma, Washington, and Rock Springs, Wyoming.

This violence had been brewing since the Chinese arrived in the United States in the 1800s. Many of these immigrants came to join the gold rush and help build the railroads. Generally, these immigrants weren't well received. Cities such as San Francisco, California, refused to allow Chinese children to attend white schools. California passed laws to tax each immigrant and tried to forbid Chinese immigrants from entering the state. In 1876, the US Supreme Court ruled that these laws were unconstitutional. But resistance toward Chinese residents continued. As the

US economy worsened, labor leaders argued that Chinese immigrants were decreasing wages and taking jobs from whites.

THE CHINESE EXCLUSION ACT AND BLACK VOTER ROLLBACK

This anti-Chinese feeling led Congress to pass the Chinese Exclusion Act in 1882. The act blocked Chinese immigrants from entering the United States. It also forbade Chinese residents from applying for citizenship. Since they weren't citizens, Chinese residents couldn't vote.

After the act passed, the US Chinese population sharply declined. Supporters of the law considered this decline a success. Other Asians living in the United States, such as Japanese, Filipino, and Indian Americans, were targeted with similar laws. As a result of these laws, Asians living in the United States couldn't become citizens and vote until 1952.

As Chinese immigrants were struggling in the West, blacks began to lose their Reconstruction voting powers in the South. The white people who had been in charge before the Civil War began to return to power. Each Southern state began stripping black men of the right to vote. However, because of the Fifteenth Amendment, the states couldn't do this openly. So they devised methods to discourage and eliminate African American voters. Throughout the South, these methods included literacy tests, poll taxes, and grandfather clauses.

A political cartoon from 1916 acknowledged the barriers that some people in the United States faced when trying to vote.

LITERACY TESTS

Literacy tests were supposed to be used when voters couldn't prove they had a certain level of education. The tests consisted of questions about state laws or general logic. They were also supposed to be given to both white and black voters. But the tests' format and questions were completely up to a white voting registrar. A white voter might be asked to explain one sentence of the state's constitution, while a black voter could be asked incredibly difficult questions in order to vote.

In Louisiana, black voters had to take a logic test. It had questions such as "draw a triangle with a blackened circle that overlaps only its left corner," and "in the space below, write the word 'noise' backwards and place a dot over what would be its second letter should it have been written forward."[2]

In Mississippi, voters were tested on the state constitution. Mississippi senator Theodore Bilbo said the constitution had been rewritten so that black men wouldn't be able to understand it. In Alabama, black voters were asked the length of the term of a US Supreme Court justice. This was a trick question, because there is no limit to a Supreme Court justice's term. Civil rights leader John Lewis later became a US Representative. He said, "You had to count the number of jelly beans in a jar or the number of bubbles in a bar of soap. Black teachers and college professors could not pass [those] literacy tests."[3]

Researcher Carol Anderson says the literacy tests were especially effective because Southern states refused to educate blacks. In 1940, more than 50 percent of black Mississippians had fewer than five years of formal education. Twelve percent of black Mississippians had no schooling at all.[4] Most Southern states also spent much more on white students. In Louisiana, white students received four times as much funding as black students.[5] Additionally, many counties in the South had no high schools for African Americans.

POLL TAXES

After Reconstruction, all states that had fought for the South in the Civil War adopted a poll tax. A poll tax required voting-age men to pay yearly to vote. Poll tax supporters argued that the funds could be used to support public schools. But data shows very little money was raised from poll taxes. In Arkansas, only 5 percent of the school budget came from poll taxes, but 80 percent of the state's eligible voters were eliminated from voting because of the tax.[6]

States could also require that the poll tax be paid to the local police. In many black communities, local sheriffs were viewed with fear. Knowing this, some sheriffs forced residents to pay them directly.

Voters also had to pay a back fee for all their eligible years of voting. So if the yearly fee was $1, a voter with 20 years of eligibility would need to pay $20 to vote. In the 1940s, the

Poll tax receipts were given to people who paid poll taxes.

National Committee to Abolish the Poll Tax estimated that ten million Americans couldn't vote because they couldn't pay the tax.[7]

Additionally, some states required that voters show receipts for two years of poll taxes. In Mississippi, white voter receipts were kept on file to make it easier for them to vote. Black voter receipts were not. The poll tax was so effective that it lowered voter turnout for all voters. In the 1944 presidential election, states with poll taxes had a turnout rate of only 18 percent.[8]

THE GRANDFATHER CLAUSE

Because literacy tests and poll taxes also affected poor whites, Southern states came up with another device to protect the white vote. The device was called the grandfather clause. It said men could vote if they had voted before 1867 or if they descended from voters who could vote at that time. Since blacks couldn't vote before the Fifteenth Amendment, this effectively allowed only white men to vote. Six Southern states passed such clauses. Many of the lawmakers who passed these laws knew they may have been unconstitutional. But they thought the laws would buy them time to register white voters before being thrown out by the courts. These clauses weren't just used in Southern states. Northern states also used them to try to keep immigrants from voting.

In 1913, the Supreme Court struck down Oklahoma's grandfather clause. The law was declared a violation of the

Fifteenth Amendment. Furthermore, the justices said that no state could use pre-Fifteenth Amendment conditions as the basis for voting rights.

THE CRASH IN BLACK VOTER RATES AND JIM CROW

All of these obstacles resulted in a huge decrease in black voters in the South. Louisiana had 130,000 blacks registered to vote in 1896. Once the new laws went into effect, that number dropped to 1,342 in 1904. This same drop occurred across the South. By 1940, only 3 percent of eligible blacks in the South were registered to vote.[9]

The Texas All-White Primary

After Reconstruction, Texas Democrats wanted to make sure black Americans and Mexican Americans couldn't participate in state politics. In 1923, the Texas Democratic party passed a law forbidding nonwhites from voting in a Democratic primary. A primary election decides who should run in a general election. This meant black and Mexican American voters would have no say in selecting the candidates who would eventually run the state. The Supreme Court struck down the 1923 law. But Texas kept trying to maintain all-white elections. This practice wouldn't end until 1944, when the Supreme Court said Texas's primaries were unconstitutional.

Antiblack voting laws were just one part of the larger effort to prevent black people from having equal rights in the South. From the end of Reconstruction in the 1870s to the mid-1960s, Southern states created a web of laws and customs known as

Into the 1960s, people were fighting to eliminate Jim Crow laws.

Jim Crow laws that put blacks on the bottom of the economic and social structure. These laws included separate bathrooms and drinking fountains from whites. They required blacks to go to separate schools and to be treated at separate hospitals.

By custom, blacks had to step off the sidewalk when a white person approached.

Any violation of the Jim Crow system could be met with violence. One of the worst incidents was the murder of Emmett Till in 1955. Emmett was a black teen from Chicago, Illinois, who was accused of whistling at a white woman in Mississippi. As punishment, a group of white men kidnapped, tortured, and then hanged him. His body was dumped in a river. Emmett's mother decided to have an open casket at his funeral to show what had been done to her son. What happened to Emmett was a rallying cry for civil rights movement.

The Continuing Impact of Lynching

In 1931, Raymond Gunn, an African American man, was chained and hanged from the roof of a schoolhouse. The schoolhouse was then set on fire. A large crowd watched as he was hanged and burned to death. Many people in the crowd were white women and children. One mother even held up her child to get a better look.

Gunn's murder is an example of a lynching, which is a killing by a mob without legal permission. In the United States, this type of mob killing often involved hangings. White mobs used these hangings to terrorize and control the black population after slavery. Researchers say 3,400 black people were lynched between 1881 and 1968.[10]

In 2018, the Senate passed a bill declaring lynching a federal hate crime. The law was passed unanimously and served as an apology for Congress's failure to act as thousands were murdered. But lynching may still be impacting black voter habits today. A 2017 Louisiana State University study discovered that counties with high lynching rates from 1882 to1930 have lower black voter registration rates.

Miguel Trujillo: Voting Rights Pioneer

Miguel Trujillo was a member of the Isleta Pueblo tribal community in New Mexico. After serving in World War II, Trujillo returned home and tried to register to vote. His registration was denied because he lived on a reservation. Trujillo decided to fight for his rights in federal court. He won his case and the right to vote in 1948. But the fight for Native voting rights wasn't over. All Native Americans wouldn't be able to vote in New Mexico until 1962.

VIOLENCE AND INTIMIDATION

Violence and intimidation were used against black voters. For instance, black voters were intimidated economically. They knew that their employers could be told if they tried to vote, and they worried about being fired. They could also lose their homes or be denied a loan if their attempt to vote was reported. Local police often threatened blacks who registered to vote. Black voters could be arrested on false charges or even beaten to discourage them from voting.

Black voters also knew they could be killed for attempting to vote. Black people had been killed in riots across the South because they had voted. Southern state officials even threatened blacks with violence. Mississippi senator Bilbo said, "If any [black person] tries to organize to vote, use the tar and feathers and don't forget the matches."[11] Bilbo was referring to a type of torture that involves pouring blistering hot tar on a person's body and then coating it in feathers.

BLACK VETERANS

Many black men served in the US army during World War I (1914–1918) and World War II (1939–1945). Many returned to the South with a desire to have all of their rights as US citizens. In fact, Mississippi senator James Vardaman said in 1917 that black soldiers would conclude that their political rights must be respected and that this would lead to disaster in the South.

Many returning black soldiers from both wars were killed in the South when they tried to assert their rights. One of these victims was Maceo Snipes. Snipes was a World War II veteran who registered and voted in Taylor County, Georgia, in 1946. He was the only black person in the county to vote. As a result, four white men shot and killed him on his porch. Despite this violence, black World War II veterans would go on to help lead the civil rights movement in the South.

DISCUSSION STARTERS

- Why do you think the federal government allowed Southern states to limit minority voting rights with racist laws?

- Why do you think Southern whites put in place so many barriers to prevent minorities from practicing their civil rights?

- Do you think anyone in the United States is intimidated into not voting today? Explain your answer.

CHAPTER FIVE

THE VOTING RIGHTS ACT

O n Sunday, March 7, 1965, black men, women, and teenagers gathered for a protest march in Selma, Alabama. The marchers, dressed in church clothes, walked peacefully across the Edmund Pettus Bridge. At the bottom of the bridge, the marchers met a wall of Alabama state troopers dressed in protective gear. An officer with a bullhorn barked at the crowd to turn back. The marchers refused to move. Suddenly, the officers attacked. They knocked marchers down with clubs and beat the people who fell to the ground. Then, tear gas was thrown into the crowd. Marchers began to cry, choke, and cough. They ran as they covered their faces with handkerchiefs. When it was over, black marchers were lying bloody on the ground beside the bridge.

Thousands of people took part in the march for African American voting rights in 1965.

Marchers on the Edmund Pettus Bridge were attacked with tear gas.

The violence happened because the black marchers wanted to be able to vote in Alabama. But the state of Alabama was willing to beat them to keep that from happening. The Selma march became known as Bloody Sunday.

That night, ABC News interrupted prime time television to show the event to millions of Americans. Civil rights leader Dr. Martin Luther King Jr. realized how powerful images of protestors being attacked would be. After Bloody Sunday, King said that they would show the United States what was happening to black people through television. Many Americans were already angry about the church bombing that killed four black girls in Alabama and at the Ku Klux Klan's murders of three voting activists. King was betting that the Bloody Sunday images would cause similar outrage.

King was correct. Just eight days after Bloody Sunday, President Lyndon B. Johnson introduced the Voting Rights Act (VRA) to Congress. Johnson said, "It is wrong—deadly wrong—to deny any of your fellow Americans the right to vote in this country."[1] Congress approved the act, and Johnson signed it into law on August 6, 1965.

Freedom Summer 1964

The summer of 1964 was known as Freedom Summer. That summer, Northern college students came to Mississippi to register voters and teach at freedom schools. Freedom schools were established to teach reading, math, and black history to thousands of black students. The schools also taught leaderships skills and the principles of the civil rights movement to encourage students to become activists. The mostly white volunteer teachers were told to expect to be arrested and to have money available to get out of jail. Other volunteers were beaten, arrested, and attacked by the Ku Klux Klan and local police.

Just one week into the program, three civil rights volunteers—James Chaney, Andrew Goodman, and Michael Schwerner—disappeared. Chaney was a black Mississippian. Goodman and Schwerner were white volunteers from New York. At the end of the summer, their bodies were found. They had been kidnapped and shot. Their murders became national news. The resulting outrage helped Congress pass the VRA and the Civil Rights Act of 1964. Despite the violence, the Freedom Summer efforts continued. Seventeen thousand black Mississippians would attempt to register to vote that year. However, state election officials accepted only 1,600 black voter registrations.[2]

First Indian American Congressperson

When Dalip Singh Saund ran for county judge in 1952, some Californians said they couldn't vote for a Hindu. Saund was born in India and had faced discrimination since he arrived in California in the 1920s. Despite these obstacles, he won his first election. After serving as a judge, he successfully ran for Congress in 1956. Saund represented California in the House of Representatives, and he was the first Indian American in that chamber of Congress. Throughout his time in Congress, he was a strong supporter of civil rights.

HOW THE VRA CHANGED VOTING RIGHTS

The VRA made changes to federal law. Literacy tests were no longer allowed, US attorneys could file lawsuits against states or counties with unfair voting practices, and local voting officials could be replaced with federal officials. The act also said federal observers could watch local elections in the South, and states with a history of unfair practices had to get permission from the Justice Department to make election changes.

According to researcher Carol Anderson, part of what made the VRA so different from previous efforts was that it was preventative. It didn't simply hope local governments would follow the law or that victims would complain. It made the federal government a supervisor of the nation's voting rights. This preventative feature of the voting rights act was called preclearance. It was the part of the law that required states with a history of unfairness toward African Americans to get permission before making electoral changes.

For example, if a state wanted a voter ID law, the state had to get permission to make the change from the US Justice Department. If the Justice Department disagreed with the change, it could block it. This is exactly what happened in 2012 when the Justice Department blocked a Texas photo ID law.

After the VRA was passed, more black people tried to participate in the election process.

Alabama, Alaska, Arizona, Georgia, Louisiana, Mississippi, South Carolina, Texas, and Virginia had to get permission for election changes such as altering early voting rules or moving polling places. Additionally, specific counties in California, Florida, New York, North Carolina, and South Dakota were also covered by the VRA. Several of these places were brought under the VRA after 1965 when the law was expanded to cover Asian Americans and Latinos.

OPPOSITION TO THE VRA

Some of the states covered under the VRA felt that it limited states' rights. In 1966, South Carolina sued over the presence of federal electors in the state. The Supreme Court disagreed with South Carolina's argument and upheld the VRA. Mississippi and Virginia challenged the preclearance power of the law. Both states argued minor changes to elections shouldn't require permission from the Justice Department. The Supreme Court rejected their arguments and again upheld the VRA.

But the argument that the VRA had gone too far wouldn't go away. Conservative politicians and lawyers believed federal government power should be limited. One of these conservative thinkers was Abigail Thernstrom, who has written several books on race in the United States and served on the US Commission on Civil Rights. Thernstrom said in 2007 that once the emergency of protecting black voters was achieved, preclearance was no longer necessary. Other conservatives working for Presidents

Richard Nixon, Ronald Reagan, and George W. Bush agreed with Thernstrom. One of those uncomfortable with the VRA was John Roberts, who was a lawyer for Reagan and became the chief justice of the Supreme Court in 2005. In the 1980s, Roberts helped write memos and opinion articles arguing for a weaker version of the VRA.

VRA SUCCESSES

According to writer Ari Berman, the number of black registered voters in the South increased from 31 percent to 73 percent in the decades after the VRA was passed.[3] Nationwide, the number of black elected officials increased from fewer than 500 to 10,500.[4] The Brennan Center, a policy and law center, called the VRA one of the most successful federal laws in the nation's history.

First Asian American Congresswoman

Patsy Mink, a Japanese American woman, started breaking barriers in 1944. Despite discrimination against Japanese Americans, in high school Mink won the office of student body president. In college, Mink protested policies that kept students of color from living with white students. The University of Nebraska responded by ending housing segregation. When medical schools rejected her because she was a woman, Mink applied to law school instead. After she became a lawyer, Hawaii tried to stop her from taking the bar exam. Again, Mink fought and won. She became the first Japanese American woman to practice law in Hawaii. In 1964, she ran for and won a US House seat representing Hawaii. She was the first Asian American women to be elected to Congress. Mink served in Congress until 1977.

The VRA also helped elect black representatives to Congress in large numbers. Black civil rights leaders such as Andrew Young and John Lewis were elected to the US House of Representatives from Southern states. When Young was elected in 1972, he became the first Southern black representative elected since 1901. The success of these black elected officials under the VRA paved the way for the country's first black president in 2009—Barack Obama. Obama himself said he may not have become president if not for the blood, sweat, tears, and deaths that led to the passage of the VRA.

EXTENDING THE VRA

When the VRA was passed, the focus was on the voting difficulties that black people experienced. But as time passed, Congress was pressured to expand the law. Activists wanted protection for language minorities such as the Spanish-speaking Mexican American population in the Southwest.

Ileana Ros-Lehtinen: First Latina Congressperson

When Ileana Ros-Lehtinen was elected to Congress in 1989 for Florida, she made history. News personality Katie Couric asked her how it felt to be the first Latina woman in Congress. Ros-Lehtinen responded, "Wow, I guess it feels good!"[5]

Ros-Lehtinen came to the United States as a child when her family fled Cuba. As an adult, Ros-Lehtinen worked as a teacher and principal until she decided to enter Florida politics. Ros-Lehtinen retired in 2018 after 20 years in Congress.

When the extension was debated, Congress heard the case of Texas farmer Modesto Rodriguez. He had lost a business loan when he started organizing to encourage Mexican Americans

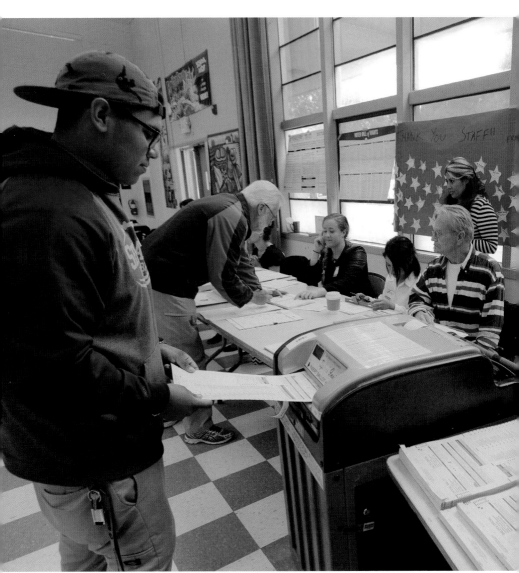

Today, US citizens of any race can vote in elections.

to vote. When he helped elect a Mexican American for mayor, the county judge had hundreds of Mexican American voters investigated. Half of their votes were later thrown out because the voters couldn't read English or write their names. Several Mexican American voters were also forced to plead guilty to election violations. According to Rodriguez, these actions helped scare Mexican Americans away from voting.

Additionally, Texas printed all election materials in English. Rodriguez said that most Mexican Americans in his town couldn't read English and 30 percent couldn't speak English either.[6] Therefore, the voting materials were like a literacy test for any voter who couldn't speak or read English. Government statistics in 1972 showed that only 44 percent of Americans with Spanish last names were registered to vote. In Texas, Mexican Americans were 16 percent of registered voters but held only 2.5 percent of elected offices.[7]

Based on all of this information, Congress passed an extension to the VRA. Under the extension, states would be covered by the VRA if more than 5 percent of voting-age residents were part of a single language minority group, if fewer than 50 percent of voting-age citizens were registered and/or voted in 1972, and if election materials were provided in English only.

These states would be required to offer all election materials in the languages of the minority groups in their states. It also brought Texas under the VRA, as it wasn't directly covered in the 1965 law. In addition, Mexicans in California, Puerto Ricans, Native Americans, Asian Americans, Alaskans, and Hawaiians became protected by the VRA. In 2015, the law was credited with increasing the number of Latinos in office. This extension was so influential that Latino activists believe that it should be celebrated as much as the original 1965 act.

DISCUSSION STARTERS

- Do you think the VRA still matters today? Explain your answer.

- Why do you think language minorities were originally overlooked by the VRA?

- Can you think of any other groups that have not been discussed that may still face obstacles to voting?

CHAPTER SIX

THE END OF THE OLD VRA

In 2012, the VRA was at the height of its power. The presidential election between President Barack Obama and Republican candidate Mitt Romney had just ended. Minority turnout was historically high.

Writer David Goldfield said this win was a direct result of the gains from the 1965 VRA. The difference in minority turnout rates gave Barack Obama a victory in the electoral college and in the popular vote. Obama also lost only one swing state—North Carolina—that he had won in 2008. The success of the VRA made black voter registration roughly equal proportionally to whites. It also relaxed or ended voting obstacles that had once lowered minority turnout. States also helped voters by adding early voting and simpler registration. VRA supporters could point to

There was a high minority voter turnout when President Barack Obama ran for reelection.

2012 as proof that the act had worked. But the moment of victory wouldn't last.

Pressure on voting rights had been mounting in the early 2000s. The 2010 midterms had elected more Republican lawmakers. The party controlled 26 state legislatures and six governors' seats. This Republican victory led to 41 states proposing bills about who could vote and how. Many of these laws were aimed at voters with low income, young people, the elderly, and minority voters. In 2011 and 2012, governors signed

Obama is a strong supporter of the Voting Rights Act.

23 laws limiting voting. Researcher Carol Anderson said, "These bills arose like dragon's teeth out of the soil of racism."[1]

SHELBY V. HOLDER (2013)

The county commissioners of Shelby County, Alabama, actively tested the limits of the VRA. They added new territory to the county and redrew boundaries in a way that limited the strength of black voters. They had done this without receiving permission from the Justice Department. In fact, the county sued the Justice Department in 2010 in hopes that the court would declare parts of the VRA unconstitutional. By the summer of 2013, the case had traveled all the way to the Supreme Court.

Four years earlier, the court had heard a similar challenge to the VRA, and the act had been upheld. But some of the justices had warned that the VRA's preclearance must be justified by current needs.

In *Shelby v. Holder,* the court ruled against the existing VRA in a 5–4 decision. The court majority said, "The VRA was unfair because it singled out and punished the South."[2] As a result, the court would cut section four of the VRA. That section decided which states and counties needed federal oversight. Without section four, the preclearance power of the VRA would no longer work. Covered states no longer needed permission to make election changes.

People waited outside the Supreme Court to hear its decision on *Shelby*.

Chief Justice John Roberts said, "In 1965 the States could be divided into those with a recent history of voting tests and low voter registration and turnout and those without those characteristics. . . . Today the Nation is no longer divided along those lines, yet the Voting Rights Act continues to treat it as if it were."[3]

Judge Ruth Bader Ginsburg was one of the four judges who disagreed. She said, "Throwing out preclearance when it has worked and is continuing to work . . . is like throwing away your umbrella in a rainstorm because you are not getting wet."[4] In just one year, the Supreme Court had weakened the VRA.

The court ruling said it was up to Congress to fix section four of the VRA. Congress would have to update the law to reflect current voting conditions. In the years since *Shelby*, bills have been introduced, but Congress hasn't passed any comprehensive fixes to the VRA.

THE REACTION

Generally, Republicans—who wanted less federal interference in state law—celebrated the change to the VRA. Conservative Edward Blum, the political activist who encouraged Shelby County officials to fight the VRA, said the law had lasted 60 years longer than intended and agreed the law had been designed for conditions that no longer existed. He argued that the original law had helped worsen the racial divide in politics.

The 2013 North Carolina Voter Law

Hours after *Shelby*, North Carolina Republicans started drafting a new voting bill. The bill shortened early voting, cut Sunday voting, and ended same-day registration. It also ended longer voting hours on Election Day and voter preregistration for people before they turned 18. The bill passed but was struck down in federal court. A federal judge said of the law, "Neither this legislature—nor, as far as we can tell, any other legislature in the country—has ever done so much, so fast, to restrict [voting] access."[5]

Democratic congressperson and activist John Lewis was saddened by the change to the VRA. He had walked across the Edmund Pettus Bridge on Bloody Sunday and been beaten down by the Alabama state police. Lewis said of *Shelby*, "These men that voted to strip the Voting Rights Act of its power, they never stood in unmovable lines, they never had to pass a so-called literacy test. It took us almost 100 years to get where we are

Jeff Sessions and Enforcing the VRA

Jeff Sessions was President Trump's attorney general from 2017 to 2018. As the country's top lawyer, Sessions was in charge of the Justice Department and determined if a state was violating the VRA. Under Sessions, Texas was able to go forward with a new voter ID law. The Obama administration said that the same ID law discriminated against racial minorities. Sessions also refused to get involved in voter redistricting cases. Sessions didn't take any new actions to protect minority voting rights while he was in office. Civil rights lawyers fear that this lack of interest in voting rights cases will harm protections for voters of color.

today. So will it take another 100 years to fix it, to change it?"[6]

2016: THE FIRST POST-SHELBY PRESIDENTIAL ELECTION

Writer Ari Berman summarized the state of voting rights in 2016 by saying, "It's easier to buy a gun than vote in many states."[7] In this post-*Shelby* environment, Republican Donald Trump beat Democrat Hillary Clinton in the 2016 presidential election. Her defeat occurred for many reasons, and voting rights experts say it's difficult to tell how many people didn't vote because of voting restrictions. As a result of the changes to the VRA, there were some notable impacts on voters of color in the 2016 election.

In areas formerly covered by the VRA, more than 850 polling places were closed.[8] These closures forced many people to travel farther from their homes to vote than in previous years.

In addition, according to the Pew Research Center, black voter turnout fell for the first time in 20 years. It went from a high of 66.6 percent in 2012 to 59.6 percent in 2016. Pew Research also said overall voter turnout fell by 2 percent.[9]

A lack of polling places makes it more difficult for people to vote.

The Latino voter turnout rate remained about the same from 2012 to 2016, with a rate of 48 percent and 47.6 percent, respectively.[10] Also, the number of eligible Latinos who don't vote stayed higher than the number of Latinos who do vote.

According to David Becker, who helped found the nonprofit Center for Election Innovation and Research, voter turnout

The For the People Act of 2019

The For the People Act was the first bill passed by the 2019 House of Representatives. If passed in the Senate, the law would impact voting rules nationwide. Some of the changes are meant to make voting easier by simplifying registration or allowing more time to vote. These changes include:

- automatic voter registration
- same-day voter registration
- 15 days of early voting
- an Election Day federal holiday

Other changes are meant to protect voters:

- using only paper voting instead of computers to prevent hacking
- reviving section four of the 1965 VRA

The law would also create new rules for removing voters from election lists and prevent state officials from making rules affecting federal elections. This act was a Democratic proposal, and it couldn't become law without the support of the 2019 Republican-controlled Senate. Senate Republican leader Mitch McConnell said the law wasn't going anywhere in the upper chamber of Congress. Republican officials and organizations disagreed with the suggested changes. They didn't want the federal government to control voter qualifications and voter rolls. They wanted states to keep these powers over elections. As of mid-2019, the act had not passed.

rates were down in the swing states of Wisconsin and Ohio. Both of these states had passed restrictive voting laws that affected minorities.

In addition, Trump and Romney carried about the same number of white voters in their respective presidential elections. But this number was enough for Trump to win in 2016. Leading up to the 2020 election, researchers were still studying how the change in the VRA affected minority voters. But all agree that the United States had a much different voting environment than prior to 2013.

DISCUSSION STARTERS

- Do you think politicians of all parties should feel a responsibility for expanding voter rights? Explain your opinion.

- Is there a need today to keep track of voting participation by race/ethnicity?

CHAPTER SEVEN

NEW OBSTACLES

During the 2014 midterms, Texas resident Mallika Das went to vote. Her son came along to help her. Das was born in India and spoke little English, which made it hard for her to vote. Her son wanted to explain the ballot to her, but an election worker stopped him. The worker said Texas law required him to be registered in the same county to help his mother. He was registered in a different county, so Das received no assistance.

Das was part of the 26 percent of Texans who spoke a language from Asia or the Pacific islands.[1] But very few Texas counties had to provide voter assistance in languages other than Spanish. The Texas law had a narrow definition for who could serve as an interpreter.

It's important that voices from people of all races are heard in elections.

RELIG
FREEDOM OF SPEECH AN
THE PRESS; THE RIGHT T
ASSEMBLE AND TO PET
THE GOVERNM
Free Expression
Witter Bynner
Native American
VOTE
Miguel Trujillo

The AALDEF works to protect the rights of Asian Americans.

The Asian American Legal Defense and Education Fund (AALDEF) sued Texas on behalf of the Das family in federal court. They argued that Texas had violated the VRA by restricting help for an English-limited voter. The Das family and AALDEF won. The ruling said a state can't limit a federal right by passing its own law with greater restrictions than the federal law. Das's voting issue is an example of the problems voters of color face in the early 2000s.

In addition to limiting assistance for non-English speakers, other hurdles people face include requiring a voter ID, limiting opportunities to vote, and preventing ex-prisoners from exercising voting rights.

According to writer Ari Berman, these obstacles are not as obvious as poll taxes and aren't limited to the South. They also don't only focus on black people. These obstacles also affect young voters, voters of color, and women voters. These are the same voters who helped Obama win in 2008 and 2012.

VOTER ID AND VOTERS OF COLOR

Voter ID laws affect Native Americans and others who have trouble getting proof of residence. They also affect other voters of color because of the cost to obtain the IDs. A Harvard University study of the states of Pennsylvania, Texas, and South Carolina recorded the costs to get a voter ID card. The study found that individuals in these states had to pay between $75 and $368.[2] In addition, the 2002 Carter-Ford Commission on Federal Election Reform estimated that 19 million potential US voters don't have a driver's license or state-issued photo ID.[3] This number includes a large amount of the young, elderly, poor, and black populations.

In Texas, the voter ID law affects many Latino voters. Texas has between 600,000 and 795,000 registered voters who have no government-issued IDs.[4] Latino voters are much more likely than white voters not to have IDs. Additionally, Texas counties with large Latino populations were less likely to have an office where residents could get an ID. Because of these concerns, the Justice Department opposed the Texas voter ID law during the Obama presidency.

Some states have laws that US citizens who want to vote must show photo IDs.

After multiple battles in federal court, Texas had to allow voters to use an alternate ID to vote, such as a military ID or birth certificate. But a lot of voters don't know about this option. The state is also supposed to host free photo ID events. But according to the Brennan Center for Justice, only one of these events was held in 2018.

Researchers have a hard time counting the number of voters affected by voter ID laws. The number of people who are stopped from voting at the polls can be counted. But it's hard to count voters who didn't show up because the law discouraged them. However, researchers have studied the Texas voter ID law. They compared two versions of the law—the 2014 version, which allowed only a state photo ID, and the 2016 law, which allowed alternate IDs. The study showed 16,000 voters would have been prevented from voting by the 2014 law. The same study also stated that 16.1 percent of Texas voters without an ID are black and 20.7 percent are Latino.[5] According to the study's authors, these numbers are evidence that voter ID laws have a greater impact on minority voters.

CLOSING POLLING PLACES AND LIMITING EARLY VOTING

When voting is inconvenient because of long lines or there are no options for voting early, some people won't vote at all. According to the Pew Research Center, 35 percent of registered voters who didn't vote in 2014 skipped voting because of scheduling.[6] It was just too hard for them to get to the polls because of work, school, or childcare commitments.

Restricting Voter Registration Groups

In 2008, Obama won approximately 70 percent of first-time voters.[7] After 2008, Republican states passed additional requirements for voter registration groups. Voter registration groups include organizations such as Rock the Vote and the League of Women Voters. These groups encourage voters to turn out, register voters, create voter guides, and may also host candidate events.

Florida was one of the states that passed new restrictions on these groups. The state required that new voter registrations be turned in within 48 hours. If registrations were late, voter groups would have to pay a large fine. The rules were so strict that the League of Women Voters stopped registering voters in Florida, calling the rules "good old-fashioned voter suppression."[8]

In Texas, volunteers can only register voters from their county. Texas also outlaws out-of-state volunteers from registering voters. Any violations of these laws can result in criminal charges.

Often, the most inconvenient voting sites are in minority communities. These voters may wait three hours or more to vote. According to a 2018 article in *USA Today*, thousands of polling places have been closed and election staffers decreased in urban and minority areas. These closures lead to longer lines at remaining voting sites. For example, in Arizona's heavily Latino Maricopa County, 2016 voters reported long lines after the jobs of hundreds of poll workers were eliminated. More recently, voters in diverse areas of New York City such as Queens and Brooklyn reported long lines at polling places for the November 2018 midterm elections. In 2012, black voters had an average wait time that was twice as long as that of whites. Florida's precincts with the highest numbers of black and Latino voters also had the longest delays.

Eliminating polling places causes confusion and discourages voters. "Any time you create additional hoops that voters have to jump through,

Souls to the Polls

Black churches have a long history of encouraging members to vote. That tradition produced Souls to the Polls. Souls to the Polls generally occurs on the last Sunday before Election Day in states that allow early voting. On this day, participating black churches encourage their members to vote after church. In southern Florida during the 2018 midterm elections, African Americans and Haitian Americans marched to the polls while music played and food was served. This tradition was so important that civil rights groups successfully pressured Florida's governor to restore Sunday voting after lawmakers dropped it. More than 800 Florida churches participated in Souls to the Polls in 2018.[9]

it hurts—particularly when it affects the poorest, most at-risk, and vulnerable citizens," said John Powers, who works with the Voting Rights Project.[10] This organization aims to help communities with low incomes, a high minority population, and people who are young or have disabilities.

At the same time polling places were closing, early voting was also decreasing. The Obama campaign successfully used early voting to increase voter turnout. In some places, Obama lost the vote on Election Day but won in early voting. After Obama's success, some Republican states rolled back early voting in 2012 and 2016. Republicans argued that cutting early voting saves money and resources. But Democrats believe that early voting is being cut because it tends to benefit Democratic candidates.

EX-PRISONERS AND VOTING RIGHTS

The majority of US states limit felons' voting rights. This puts the United States out of step with the rest of the world. Researchers estimate 6.1 million Americans couldn't vote in 2016 because of a felony.[11] This is the largest single group of Americans who can't vote. Since African Americans compose a large share of the prison population, this means 2.2 million blacks can't vote. In some states—such as Florida, Kentucky, Tennessee, and Virginia—as many as one in five black voters can't vote because of a felony conviction.[12]

Laws preventing ex-felons from voting could have a greater effect on elections than voter ID laws. The votes of ex-prisoners could make a difference in swing states such as Florida. Some researchers estimate Obama could have increased his Florida win by 2.6 points with the help of votes from ex-felons.[13] Before 2018, 1.5 million Floridians couldn't vote because of a felony.[14] Even after release, they could only vote if the governor restored their rights.

But things are changing in Florida. In November 2018, Florida voters passed an amendment to the state's constitution. It allows people with felonies to vote after they serve their sentences.

 As of mid-2019, only Vermont and Maine allowed all prisoners to vote in elections.

Both Democratic and Republican groups supported the amendment. It was passed by 64 percent of Florida voters.[15]

After the law passed, the two political parties fought over how to implement it. Republicans argued the definition of sentence completion was unclear. They added language to the law requiring all fines be paid before registering to vote. Democratic lawmakers said the law was already clear. They accused Republicans of creating a poll tax to restore voting rights.

As late as 2019, ex-felons were unsure if they could legally register to vote or not. One ex-prisoner said she owed as much as $190,000 and may never be able to vote if all fines have to be paid first.[16]

FEELINGS TOWARD VOTING RESTRICTIONS

People note that there are different reasons for limiting voting rights. In 1980, conservative Paul Weyrich famously said, "I don't want everybody to vote. Elections are not won by a majority

of the people, they never have been from the beginning of the country and they are not now."[17]

Many conservatives feel voting is more of a privilege than a right. They agree with Weyrich and the Founding Fathers that some restrictions are better for the country. Conservative writer Jonah Goldberg said in 2005, "People who want to make voting easier are in effect saying that those who previously didn't care or know enough about the country to vote are exactly the kind of voters this country needs now."[18]

On the other hand, liberal politicians such as 2020 presidential candidate Senator Bernie Sanders argue against voting limitations. In fact, Sanders stated that even people in jail should still be able to exercise the right to vote. Sanders said, "I think the right to vote is inherent in our democracy."[19]

DISCUSSION STARTERS

- How easy should it be for people to vote?

- Do you think ex-prisoners should be able to vote after they serve their time? Explain your opinion.

- Do you believe that voting is a right or privilege? Explain your opinion.

CHAPTER EIGHT

GERRYMANDERING AND POLITICAL POWER

I n 1788, two Founding Fathers were locked in a battle.
Virginia governor Patrick Henry wanted revenge on his rival
and future president, James Madison. Henry convinced the
Virginia legislature to draw the fifth congressional district so
Madison would have to beat the toughest political opponent
to win the seat. Henry knew that controlling the district's
boundary lines could help determine who won the election.
Henry's plan failed—Madison went on to become a member of
Congress. However, Henry's idea to weaken the people's voting
power by playing with a district's boundaries is still part of
US politics today.

Playing with the size and shape of a district to get an
advantage during elections is called *gerrymandering*. This is
more than just redistricting—when districts are redrawn every

People have protested gerrymandering.

STOP VOTER
SUPPRESSION
AND
ERRYMANDERING
WE
DEMAND SAFE
SECURE
ELECTIONS 4 ALL

The word *gerrymandering* comes from Founding Father Elbridge Gerry. He was known for intelligence, hard work, and stubbornness. He went on to become governor of Massachusetts and vice president of the United States.

While governor, Gerry signed a redistricting law. Opponents complained that the new district was unnatural and mangled. They called the odd-shaped district a *Gerry-mander* because it looked like a salamander. A drawing called the "Gerry-mander" appeared in an 1812 edition of the *Boston Gazette*. The term has been a part of politics ever since.

ten years according to new census data. It's about changing a district's boundaries for maximum advantage. President Benjamin Harrison called it "political robbery."[1]

According to Anderson, the political party in charge gets to redraw districts to their advantage. This process takes place every ten years and relies on census data. But taken to extremes, it creates districts in which the winner can be determined before any votes are cast.

This type of extreme redistricting sparked the *Economist* newspaper's Intelligence Unit to list the United States as a "flawed democracy."[2] There are three types of gerrymandering: racial gerrymandering, partisan gerrymandering, and prison gerrymandering.

RACIAL GERRYMANDERING

Racial gerrymandering is drawing districts around racial groups. For example, sometimes communities of blacks or Latinos are split into separate districts to minimize their voting power. Courts have stepped in to block these actions.

Voters of color can also be put together to allow them to elect their own representatives. In the 1990s, black Democrats and Republicans partnered to create majority-black districts in the South. This process elected Southern blacks to Congress in large numbers for the first time since Reconstruction. In the past, courts have been mixed about whether this is acceptable.

PARTISAN GERRYMANDERING

According to the Brennan Center for Justice, partisan gerrymandering occurs when a political party uses this process to artfully craft maps that lock in an outsized share of seats for an entire decade. However, since Democratic voters and voters of color are often contained in large urban areas, partisan gerrymandering may overlap with racial gerrymandering.

In 2010, Republicans took control of 26 state governments. This gave them authority to recreate congressional boundaries in those states to their benefit. For example, Republican consultant Thomas Hofeller became famous for using software to create ideal districts for Republican candidates in North Carolina. The software used neighborhood population data—including racial makeup—to maximize the number of Republican voters in each district. Hofeller was so effective that even after his death, his redistricting work remained the subject of federal lawsuits. However, Republicans aren't the only ones engaging in this

Using Math to Solve Gerrymandering

Computer formulas helped create drastically gerrymandered districts. Therefore, mathematicians argue these formulas can also create fair districts. A database of fair maps can be developed. Using a mathematical formula, any proposed map can be compared against the database. Extreme maps will look like points at the end of a bell curve.

Supreme Court Chief Justice John Roberts and Justice Neil Gorsuch have shown discomfort with using formulas to determine if a district is too extreme. But the state of Pennsylvania has successfully used this approach to help decide whether a proposed district is fair. Additionally, Missouri voters supported a constitutional amendment in 2018 requiring mathematical rules to ensure district fairness. However, as of 2019, Missouri's Republican governor was pushing to repeal the law.

extreme redistricting. Democrats in Illinois and Maryland worked just as hard to eliminate Republican-held districts in their states. As of 2019, the Supreme Court decided that the federal courts should not have any say in gerrymandering. Congress and the individual states will have to determine what the rules for the process should be going forward.

THE EXTREME SHAPES OF REDISTRICTING

According to Carol Anderson, after the 2010 elections, "states began to have districts that looked like contorted yoga positions."[3] These odd districts were given nicknames such as "the North Carolina Gimpy Leg," "the Texas Glock," and "the Georgia Flat Cat Road Kill."[4] In Ohio, parts of Toledo and Cleveland were connected by a beach around Lake Erie to force two Democrats to battle for one seat.

In North Carolina, partisan gerrymandering meant that districts were redrawn so that the colleges around Raleigh and Durham were scooped out of the surrounding suburbs. Then a sliver of the same district stretched south to Fayetteville. The headline of a *Washington Post* article said North Carolina's districts are so misshapen they look like monsters.

Democrats have sued in Texas and North Carolina when they believed districts were drawn to intentionally decrease minority voting power. They also formed groups in California and Florida to pressure legislators not to draw overly partisan districts. Despite these efforts, more Americans live in uncompetitive districts. Researcher and London School of Economics Fellow Brian Klaas said, "In 2016, there were no truly competitive Congressional races in 42 of the 50 states. That is not healthy for

Professor David Niven of the University of Cincinnati, Ohio, shows a map of a gerrymandered area in the state.

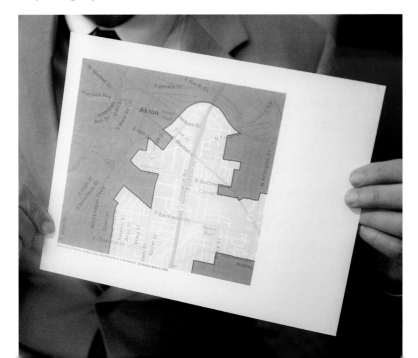

a system of government that, at its core, is defined by political competition."[5]

PRISON GERRYMANDERING

US districts are also affected by the way the US census counts prisoners. In 2019, many states allowed prisoners to be counted as residents of the city where they were jailed. But they aren't true residents of these cities. When the prisoners leave jail, they often leave the city. Thus, cities and counties gain greater political representation from their prison populations, even though those prisoners will likely never live or vote in those communities.

Generally, prison populations have large numbers of people who are black and Latino. But the prisons where they are held are in white, rural areas. So these areas are benefitting from blacks and Latinos who are jailed there but can't vote there. The civil rights group National Association for the Advancement of Colored People (NAACP) argues that this practice is unconstitutional.

EFFECTS ON VOTER TURNOUT

All of this manipulation is bad for voter participation. In 2016, black voter turnout decreased in every state with radically redrawn districts. The process also diminished the impact of Latino voters in elections. Additionally, when districts are less competitive, all voters are more likely to stay away from the polls. This means that elections are less likely to bring about change.

Klaas wrote in the *Washington Post* that he believes this process of redistricting has broken US democracy.

In 2018, Democrats won 40 seats to retake control of the US House of Representatives. Their win was called a blue wave. But experts say the win was smaller than it could have been because of gerrymandering. In North Carolina, Democrats won 50 percent of the vote but could only win three of 13 congressional races.[6] North Carolina also had some of the most gerrymandered districts in the country. Democrats were spread too thin in most of the state's districts to win.

Ohio is another state with extreme districts. Democrats also had trouble there. They didn't win any additional House seats, even though they won almost half of the state vote. In contrast, Democrats did well in Pennsylvania. They gained four seats in 2018. But in Pennsylvania, the state Supreme Court redrew the Republican gerrymandered districts.

DISCUSSION STARTERS

- Do you think gerrymandering is fair in any type of situation? Explain your opinion.
- Do you think prisoners should be counted as residents of the town where they're imprisoned? Explain your answer.
- Why do you think gerrymandering can discourage people from voting?

CHAPTER NINE

THE TRUMP ERA

President Donald Trump's election in 2016 occurred during a time of deep political and racial divisions in the United States. These divisions could be seen in data showing party support by race. According to a 2017 Pew Research study, 84 percent of African Americans called themselves Democrats. The same study found that approximately two-thirds of Latinos and Asians leaned Democratic and 51 percent of white voters leaned Republican.[1] The Pew study also found that Americans were so divided that they were less likely to marry or even be friends with people they disagreed with. Only 14 percent of Republicans said they had Democratic friends, and only 9 percent of Democrats said they had Republican friends.[2]

Some people are very outspoken about laws that could restrict people's ability to vote.

This divided era also provided new challenges for voters of color. Three events illustrate some of these challenges: the 2017 special election of Senator Doug Jones in Alabama, the 2018 Georgia governor's race, and the voter fraud claims by Trump in the 2016 and 2018 elections.

THE 2017 SPECIAL ELECTION OF ALABAMA SENATOR DOUG JONES

"Voting has always been burdensome for black people in Alabama," said journalist Vann R. Newkirk II.[3] Alabama doesn't allow early voting, absentee voting, preregistration for 17-year-olds, or same-day registration. Alabama also passed a strict voter ID law in 2011—only state photo IDs were accepted. The 2011 law was so strict that state legislators shelved it, knowing that it couldn't survive Justice Department review. It only became law after the 2013 *Shelby* decision ended the preclearance section of the VRA. The law required acquiring a state ID from the Department of Motor Vehicles (DMV). The state also said voters could go online to get IDs. But many black people who lived in rural areas didn't have internet access. Additionally, there were more than 200,000 ex-felons living in Alabama whose voting rights had been restored by state law in 2017.[4] But those ex-felons had never been notified that they could vote.

Despite all of this, Democrat Doug Jones won the special election for the Senate in 2017. Jones ran against a Republican

Since Doug Jones won in a special election, he would have to
campaign again in the 2020 race to keep his seat.

candidate with a damaged reputation. The Republican

opponent, Roy Moore, had been accused of engaging in sexual

misconduct with underage girls. Black voters were given the

credit for Jones's win. More black voters had turned out for Jones

(29 percent) than had turned out to vote for Obama in 2012

(26 percent).[5]

Specifically, Jones won because of efforts to increase black turnout. These efforts included statewide rallies to get out the vote, legal clinics and radio ads to let ex-felons know they could vote, one-on-one contact with voters through phone calls and door-to-door visits, voter ID clinics to help voters get the right ID, and volunteer transportation to the polls. The outcome of Jones's election showed that focused efforts to get out the minority vote could work even in a state where voting was difficult for African Americans.

THE 2018 GEORGIA GOVERNOR'S RACE

More than one week after a close 2018 election, Democratic candidate Stacey Abrams faced TV cameras. She admitted her opponent, Brian Kemp, would become Georgia's next governor. But Abrams also declared that "democracy failed Georgia."[6]

Abrams was upset because of Kemp's actions as Georgia's secretary of state. In the months leading up to the election, Kemp purged, or eliminated, 85,000 people from Georgia's voter lists. In 2017 overall, approximately 668,000 Georgia voters were cut. After looking at the numbers, Greg Palast, an investigative reporter, said that 340,134 people shouldn't have been removed from the list.[7]

Federal law requires that voter rolls be checked for ineligible voters. These ineligible voters include people with name changes who haven't notified officials, people who died, people who moved away, and people who committed a felony. States are then supposed to contact these voters. If the voter doesn't respond, they can be cut. However, in Georgia and other states, voters are cut simply for not voting recently. This affects minority, poor, and young voters more than other voters. These same voters tend to lean Democrat when they do vote. Republicans say that they are following the law with voter purges and are only seeking to prevent voter fraud.

Voting rights activists believe voter purges are efforts to limit minority and Democratic turnout. NAACP president Derrick Johnson said of the Georgia election, "Kemp's actions during the election were textbook voter suppression. His actions were strategic, careless and aimed at silencing the voting power of communities of color in the state."[8]

Fair Fight Action

After losing the Georgia governor's race, Stacey Abrams started a group called Fair Fight Action. The group focuses on election reform, voter turnout, and voter education to improve voting conditions in Georgia. The group will also file lawsuits when it feels the state has mismanaged elections. Abrams even appeared in a 2019 Super Bowl ad for the group to promote free and fair elections.

In Georgia, Kemp also used a process called exact match to deny 53,000 voter registrations. Seventy percent of denied registrations were from African Americans.[9] Exact match requires that registration forms match Social Security and driver's license records. If a name is misspelled or missing a middle name or hyphen, the registration can be blocked. Further, if voters didn't correct their registration within 40 days, their registrations were canceled. Kemp's office was sued twice over its exact match policy. In 2016, activists filed the first suit, saying the process unnecessarily targeted voters of color and confused voters. This case was settled in 2017 after Kemp's office agreed to allow those canceled to vote if they provided ID at the polls. In the fall of 2018, another group of civil rights activists sued to end the exact match program.

ISSUES OF FAIRNESS

Because Kemp was secretary of state, he was in charge of the state's election rules. Democrats felt he had tightened election rules and cut voters in order to win. Kemp said he had done nothing wrong and suggested Abrams was trying to undermine democracy and steal the election by making charges against him.

In 2018, three secretaries of state were in charge of their own statewide elections. All three were accused of limiting voter access. There's no rule against running for office while supervising a state's electoral process in the United States. But many other countries have professionals who aren't tied to either political party run elections.

Kemp beat Abrams by a little more than 50,000 votes—or 1.4 percent.[10] In March 2019, House Democrats announced they would investigate whether he had wrongly limited voter access. As of mid-2019, there was no final report on the investigation.

DONALD TRUMP AND CLAIMS OF FRAUD

Throughout his 2016 presidential campaign, Trump talked about voter fraud. He mentioned this often on Twitter and at rallies. "I'm afraid the election is going to be rigged, I have to be honest," Trump said.[11] Despite his fears, Trump went on to win the presidential election.

Because of Trump's claims, the *Washington Post* examined news reports nationwide for evidence of voter fraud. They found only four examples in the 2016 election, and there was no evidence that cheating had affected the 2016 vote counts.

In 2017, Trump created the Presidential Advisory Commission on Election Integrity. One of his commission members said they found no evidence of voter fraud. After just seven months, Trump ended the commission without any proof for his claims.

Heritage Foundation Voter Fraud Database

Republicans who are concerned about voter fraud rely on a database run by the Heritage Foundation. The group keeps a state-by-state list of more than 1,100 instances of fraud.[12] It lists different types of voter fraud, such as altering vote count and duplicate voting. It also lists whether the case ended up in civil or criminal court. Critics say this list goes back to 1948 and has only 105 cases of fraud since 2013.[13]

Voting rights were expected to be discussed as the 2020 presidential election drew near.

CLAIMS OF NONCITIZEN VOTING

Trump isn't alone in claiming cases of voter fraud. Since the beginning of the 2000s, several Republican-led states have claimed that large numbers of noncitizens were voting. In 2012, Florida officials said 180,000 noncitizens had registered. But after the state researched the list, the number shrank to 85. That same

year, Michigan said 4,000 noncitizens had registered. But only 10 out of the 4,000 were suspected of actually voting illegally.[14]

Trump also said he was the victim of noncitizen voting. However, researchers have found very little proof of noncitizen voting. A 2017 Brennan Center for Justice study found only 30 noncitizen voting incidents out of 23 million votes.[15]

More than three million people live in the US territory of Puerto Rico and are considered US citizens.[16] The island is a US territory and abides by federal laws. However, as of 2019, they couldn't vote for president or their own Congress representative or senator. If residents of Puerto Rico want to have full citizenship rights, they have to move to the US mainland. Some Puerto Ricans argue this is unfair. "What compelling argument could support policies that deprive us of these fundamental rights?" said lawyer Gregorio J. Igartua.[17]

This lack of voting power gained attention after Puerto Rico was struck by a major hurricane in 2017. Puerto Ricans had to fight the US government for more funds to rebuild. But they were at a disadvantage because they had no legislators with full voting power to push for funding. Additionally, even some government officials seemed confused about Puerto Rico's status. A White House official twice referred to Puerto Rico as "that country."[18]

In 2018, Puerto Rico's governor, Ricardo Rosselló, joined an effort to pressure the United States to give full citizenship rights to Puerto Ricans. Some of the island's leaders have been asking for the opportunity to become a US state since the 1960s. As of 2019, Puerto Rico had held multiple votes asking people there if they wanted the island to become a US state. In 2017, the majority of Puerto Ricans who voted said they wanted to—though voter turnout was low. However, as of mid-2019, Puerto Rico remained a US territory. A group of current and former government officials argued that the United States violates international human rights laws by denying Puerto Ricans full voting rights.

In 2019, US lawmakers proposed legislation to make Puerto Rico a US state. Ricardo Rosselló, *pictured*, Puerto Rico's governor at the time, was a supporter of statehood for the island.

Nonetheless, concerns surrounding noncitizen voting popped up again in the 2018 midterms. Texas Republicans said 58,000 noncitizens voted and 95,000 noncitizens registered.[19] However, an adviser from the Texas Department of Elections said further research was needed to prove the claim. The numbers came from state data that showed 95,000 people had shown noncitizen IDs to get a driver's license or personal identification card. Fifty-eight thousand from this group had also voted in Texas at least once since 1996. But these residents could have signed up for Texas driver's licenses before they became US citizens. Therefore, the 58,000 residents could have all been citizens by the time they voted.

In 2019, the League of United Latin American Citizens sued Texas over the noncitizen voting claims. The group said the claims amounted to illegal voter intimidation. Specifically, they accused state officials of misstating noncitizen voting numbers to discourage Latinos from voting and to enlist the public to help in that effort.

Researchers have investigated how these claims affect Latino voters. In 2017 the Public Religion Research Institute and the *Atlantic* magazine conducted a study of voting barriers faced by black and Latino voters. The study found that one in ten Latinos reported being harassed at the polls in 2016.[20] Sociology and Immigration Studies professor Robert Courtney Smith said that Latino voters are perceived as undocumented immigrants. This perception denies them the legitimacy that other citizens enjoy and creates an unwelcoming climate when they try to vote.

The United States continues to struggle with voting rights and has not yet resolved how far it should go to protect people's right to vote. Additionally, voter ID, partisan gerrymandering, and voting rights for ex-felons will help impact how many voters of color turn out for the 2020 elections. These issues will help decide the winners of the 2020 congressional and presidential elections. The important story of the United States' voting history and its connection to race is far from over.

DISCUSSION STARTERS

- Brainstorm some effective methods for encouraging voter turnout. Explain why your methods would work.

- Do you think people in the United States should be concerned with voter fraud during elections? Explain your opinion.

- Do you think having restrictions on US citizens voting is fair? Explain your answer.

ESSENTIAL FACTS

SIGNIFICANT EVENTS

- The Fifteenth Amendment was ratified in 1870 to ensure that African Americans had voting rights. However, the amendment didn't provide voting rights for Native Americans, Asian Americans, or women.

- After Reconstruction ended, Southern states passed a series of laws restricting blacks' voting power. These laws were enforced with violence and intimidation for decades.

- Native Americans received citizenship through the 1924 Indian Citizenship Act.

- The Voting Rights Act was passed in 1965 to end Southern obstacles to black voting rights. In 1975, the Voting Rights Act protections were extended to cover language minorities, including Spanish-speaking Latino Americans.

- In 2013, the Supreme Court ended part of the Voting Rights Act in *Shelby v. Holder*. US jurisdictions with a history of voter discrimination no longer had to ask the Department of Justice for permission before changing voting laws.

- In 2018, the Georgia governor's race drew widespread attention. Secretary of State Brian Kemp, a Republican candidate and ultimate winner of the race, cut tens of thousands of Georgians from the voter rolls.

KEY PLAYERS

- President Barack Obama was reelected in 2012 with big turnout numbers from voters of color.

- In 2013, Supreme Court chief justice John Roberts wrote the majority decision regarding changing the Voting Rights Act of 1965.

- After Obama's reelection, Republican state legislators began to pass new voter restrictions, making voting harder for people of color.

- Donald Trump won the presidency in 2016 and raised concerns about high levels of voter fraud.

IMPACT ON SOCIETY

Many people view voting as an essential right for citizens of the United States. Throughout the years, many minority groups have struggled to obtain the ability to vote. Practices such as gerrymandering and voter roll cuts continue to threaten people's voting rights and power.

QUOTE

"These men that voted to strip the Voting Rights Act of its power, they never stood in unmovable lines, they never had to pass a so-called literacy test. It took us almost 100 years to get where we are today. So will it take another 100 years to fix it, to change it?"

—*Democratic member of Congress and activist John Lewis on the 2013 change to the VRA*

GLOSSARY

absentee voting

The ability to cast a vote through the mail instead of at the polls.

advocate

A person who actively supports a cause, policy, or group.

civil rights

A guarantee of equal social opportunities and equal protection under the law, regardless of gender, race, religion, or other personal traits.

Confederate

Having to do with the culture or beliefs of the former Confederate States of America.

conservative

A person who believes in small government and established social, economic, and political traditions and practices.

discriminate

To judge a person positively or negatively on the basis of race, class, sex, or other category.

early voting

When qualified people can vote before Election Day.

incumbent

Someone who currently holds public office.

liberal

A person who believes in large government and supports new ideas and ways of behaving.

literacy

The ability to read or write.

oversight

Refers to reviewing and monitoring by a branch of government or a government agency.

preregistration

A process that lets underage people register to vote so they can participate in elections as soon as they become 18 years old.

same-day registration

To register to vote on Election Day.

ADDITIONAL RESOURCES

SELECTED BIBLIOGRAPHY

Anderson, Carol. *One Person, No Vote: How Voter Suppression Is Destroying Our Democracy.* Bloomsbury, 2018.

Berman, Ari. *Give Us the Ballot: The Modern Struggle for Voting Rights in America.* Farrar, Straus and Giroux, 2015.

Gamboa, Suzanne. "For Latinos, 1965 Voting Rights Act Impact Came a Decade Later." *NBC News*, 6 Aug. 2015, nbcnews.com. Accessed 16 May 2019.

FURTHER READINGS

Harris, Duchess. *Reconstructing the South.* Abdo, 2020.

Harris, Duchess. *The Right to Vote.* Abdo, 2018.

ONLINE RESOURCES

To learn more about voting, race, and the law, please visit **abdobooklinks.com** or scan this QR code. These links are routinely monitored and updated to provide the most current information available.

MORE INFORMATION

For more information on this subject, contact or visit the following organizations:

AMERICAN CIVIL LIBERTIES UNION (ACLU)

125 Broad St., Eighteenth Floor
New York, NY 10004
212-549-2500

aclu.org

By working through legislatures, courts, and communities, the ACLU works to defend US citizens' rights.

BRENNAN CENTER FOR JUSTICE

120 Broadway, Suite 1750
New York, NY 10271
646-292-8310

brennancenter.org

The Brennan Center for Justice focuses on defending, reforming, and adjusting US democratic and justice systems. One area the center focuses on is the right to vote.

SOURCE NOTES

CHAPTER 1. NATIVE AMERICANS AND VOTING RIGHTS

1. "North Dakota Presidential Race Results: Donald J. Trump Wins." *New York Times*, 1 Aug. 2017, nytimes.com. Accessed 1 Aug. 2019.

2. John Nichols. "Will North Dakota's Discriminatory Voter-ID Law Cost Democrats the Senate?" *Nation*, 15 Oct. 2018, thenation.com. Accessed 1 Aug. 2019.

3. "14th Amendment." *Cornell Law School*, n.d., law.cornell.edu. Accessed 1 Aug. 2019.

4. Becky Little. "Native Americans Weren't Guaranteed the Right to Vote in Every State Until 1962." *History*, 6 Nov. 2018, history.com. Accessed 1 Aug. 2019.

5. Mica Rosenberg. "Native Americans Move to Frontlines in Battle over Voting Rights." *Reuters*, 31 May 2016, reuters.com. Accessed 1 Aug. 2019.

6. Amy Dalrymple. "Native Voting Rights Group Aims to Remove Hurdles in North Dakota." *Bismarck Tribune*, 12 Oct. 2018, bismarcktribune.com. Accessed 1 Aug. 2019.

7. Ashoka Mukpo. "Supreme Court Enables Mass Disenfranchisement of North Dakota's Native Americans." *ACLU*, 12 Oct. 2018, aclu.org. Accessed 1 Aug. 2019.

8. "North Dakota Senate: Cramer vs. Heitkamp." *Real Clear Politics*, n.d., realclearpolitics.com. Accessed 1 Aug. 2019.

CHAPTER 2. THE LONG PATH TO THE BLACK MAN'S VOTE

1. Ed Crews. "Voting in Early America." *Colonial Williamsburg*, spring 2007, history.org. Accessed 1 Aug. 2019.

2. Crews, "Voting in Early America."

3. "Mayflower Compact." *History*, 29 Oct. 2009, history.com. Accessed 1 Aug. 2019.

4. "Mayflower Compact."

5. Kat Eschner. "For a Few Decades in the 18th Century, Women and African-Americans Could Vote in New Jersey." *Smithsonian Magazine*, 16 Nov. 2017, smithsonianmag.com. Accessed 1 Aug. 2019.

6. "Black Residents of Nashville to the Union Convention." *Freedmen & Southern Society Project*, n.d., freedmen.umd.edu. Accessed 1 Aug. 2019.

7. Mark Leibovich. "Rights vs. Rights: An Improbable Collision Course." *New York Times*, 13 Jan. 2008, nytimes.com. Accessed 1 Aug. 2019.

8. Leibovich, "Rights vs. Rights."

9. Frederick Douglass. "An Appeal to Congress for Impartial Suffrage." *Atlantic*, n.d., theatlantic.com. Accessed 1 Aug. 2019.

10. "Women's Suffrage: Their Rights and Nothing Less." *Library of Congress*, n.d., loc.gov. Accessed 1 Aug. 2019.

CHAPTER 3. RECONSTRUCTION AND BLACK VOTING POWER

1. Eric Foner. "South Carolina's Forgotten Black Political Revolution." *Slate*, 31 Jan. 2018, slate.com. Accessed 1 Aug. 2019.

2. Laine Kaplan-Levenson. "An Absolute Massacre: The 1866 Riot at the Mechanics' Institute." *New Orleans Public Radio*, 14 July 2016, wwno.org. Accessed 1 Aug. 2019.

CHAPTER 4. VOTING RIGHTS ROLLBACK

1. Phil Dougherty. "Mobs Forcibly Expel Most of Seattle's Chinese Residents Beginning on February 7, 1886." *History Link*, 17 Nov. 2013, historylink.org. Accessed 1 Aug. 2019.

2. Rebecca Onion. "Take the Impossible 'Literacy' Test Louisiana Gave Black Voters in the 1960s." *Slate*, 28 June 2013, slate.com. Accessed 1 Aug. 2019.

3. Charles E. Cobb Jr. "The Voting Rights Act, 45 Years Later." *Root*, 6 Aug. 2010, theroot.com. Accessed 1 Aug. 2019.

4. Carol Anderson. *One Person, No Vote: How Voter Suppression Is Destroying Our Democracy*. Bloomsbury, 2018. 5.

5. Anderson, *One Person, No Vote*, 5.

6. Anderson, *One Person, No Vote*, 8.

7. Anderson, *One Person, No Vote*, 9.

8. Anderson, *One Person, No Vote*, 10.

9. Anderson, *One Person, No Vote*, 4.

10. Jamiles Lartey and Same Morris. "How White Americans Used Lynchings to Terrorize and Control Black People." *Guardian*, 26 Apr. 2018, theguardian.com. Accessed 1 Aug. 2019.

11. Anderson, *One Person, No Vote*, 15.

CHAPTER 5. THE VOTING RIGHTS ACT

1. Ari Berman. *Give Us the Ballot: The Modern Struggle for Voting Rights in America*. Farrar, Straus and Giroux, 2015. 5–6.

2. "Freedom Summer." *Stanford University*, n.d., kinginstitute.stanford.edu. Accessed 1 Aug. 2019.

3. Berman, *Give Us the Ballot*, 240.

4. Berman, *Give Us the Ballot*, 240.

5. Ashlee Anderson. "Ileana Ros-Lehtinen." *National Women's History Museum*, n.d., womenshistory.org. Accessed 1 Aug. 2019.

6. Ari Berman. "The Lost Promise of the Voting Rights Act." *Atlantic*, 5 Aug. 2015, theatlantic.com. Accessed 1 Aug. 2019.

7. Berman, "The Lost Promise of the Voting Rights Act."

CHAPTER 6. THE END OF THE OLD VRA

1. Carol Anderson. *One Person, No Vote: How Voter Suppression Is Destroying Our Democracy*. Bloomsbury, 2018. 63.

2. Anderson, *One Person, No Vote*, 42.

3. Ari Berman. *Give Us the Ballot: The Modern Struggle for Voting Rights in America*. Farrar, Straus and Giroux, 2015. 9.

4. Vann R. Newkirk II. "How Shelby County v. Holder Broke America." *Atlantic*, 10 July 2018, theatlantic.com. Accessed 1 Aug. 2019.

5. William Wan. "Inside the Republican Creation of the North Carolina Voting Bill Dubbed the 'Monster' Law." *Washington Post*, 2 Sept. 2016, washingtonpost.com. Accessed 1 Aug. 2019.

6. Melissa Jeltsen. "John Lewis on Voting Rights Act: Supreme Court 'Put a Dagger in the Heart' of the Law." *HuffPost*, 25 June 2013, huffpost.com. Accessed 1 Aug. 2019.

7. Ari Berman. "Welcome to the First Presidential Election Since Voting Rights Act Gutted." *Rolling Stone*, 23 June 2016, rollingstone.com. Accessed 1 Aug. 2019.

8. Ari Berman. "There Are 868 Fewer Places to Vote in 2016 Because the Supreme Court Gutted the Voting Rights Act." *Nation*, 4 Nov. 2014, thenation.com. Accessed 1 Aug. 2019.

9. Jens Manuel Krogstad and Mark Hugo Lopez. "Black Voter Turnout Fell in 2016, Even as a Record Number of Americans Cast Ballots." *Pew Research Center*, 12 May 2017, pewresearch.org. Accessed 1 Aug. 2019.

10. Krogstad and Lopez, "Black Voter Turnout Fell in 2016."

CHAPTER 7. NEW OBSTACLES

1. Alexa Ura. "Texas Voting Law on Language Interpreters Violates Voting Rights Act, Court Says." *Texas Tribune*, 17 Aug. 2017, texastribune.org. Accessed 1 Aug. 2019.

2. "'Free' Voter IDs Are Costly, Harvard Law Report Finds." *Harvard Law Today*, 26 June 2014, today.law.harvard.edu. Accessed 1 Aug. 2019.

3. Carol Anderson. *One Person, No Vote: How Voter Suppression Is Destroying Our Democracy*. Bloomsbury, 2018. 52.

4. Ari Berman. *Give Us the Ballot: The Modern Struggle for Voting Rights in America*. Farrar, Straus and Giroux, 2015. 266.

5. Dan Hopkins. "What We Know about Voter ID Laws." *FiveThirtyEight*, 21 Aug. 2018, fivethirtyeight.com. Accessed 1 Aug. 2019.

6. Sarah Jackel and Stuart A. Thompson. "The Myth of the Lazy Nonvoter." *New York Times*, n.d., nytimes.com. Accessed 1 Aug. 2019.

7. "First-Time Voters Go Big for Obama." *ABC News*, 21 Oct. 2008, abcnews.go.com. Accessed 16 Oct. 2019.

8. Ari Berman. "A Recent History of GOP Voter Suppression in Florida." *Nation*, 1 Oct. 2012, thenation.com. Accessed 1 Aug. 2019.

9. Alex Daugherty and Lesley Clark. "Gillum Confident 'Souls to the Polls' Will Give Democrats the Early-Vote Advantage." *Miami Herald*, 4 Nov. 2018, miamiherald.com. Accessed 1 Aug. 2019.

10. Mark Nichols. "Closed Voting Sites Hit Minority Counties Harder for Busy Midterm Elections." *USA Today*, 30 Oct. 2018, usatoday.com. Accessed 1 Aug. 2019.

11. Elena Holodny. "Millions of American Adults Are Not Allowed to Vote—and They Could Change History." *Business Insider*, 3 Jan. 2018, businessinsider.com. Accessed 1 Aug. 2019.

12. Holodny, "Millions of American Adults Are Not Allowed to Vote."

13. Harry J. Enten. "Felon Voting Rights Have a Bigger Impact on Elections Than Voter ID Laws." *Guardian*, 31 July 2013, theguardian.com. Accessed 1 Aug. 2019.

14. Tim Mak. "Over 1 Million Florida Felons Win Right to Vote with Amendment 4." *NPR*, 7 Nov. 2018, npr.org. Accessed 1 Aug. 2019.

15. Mak, "Over 1 Million Florida Felons Win Right to Vote."

16. Amy Gardner. "Florida Agreed to Let Felons Vote. Now Republicans Are Trying to Limit Who Is Eligible." *Washington Post*, 26 Mar. 2019, washingtonpost.com. Accessed 1 Aug. 2019.

17. Berman, *Give Us the Ballot*, 260.

18. Zachary Roth. "The Conservative Case to Limit Voting." *MSNBC*, 18 Feb. 2014, msnbc.com. Accessed 1 Aug. 2019.

19. Sydney Ember and Matt Stevens. "Bernie Sanders Opens Space for Debate on Voting Rights for Incarcerated People." *New York Times*, 27 Apr. 2019, nytimes.com. Accessed 1 Aug. 2019.

CHAPTER 8. GERRYMANDERING AND POLITICAL POWER

1. Carol Anderson. *One Person, No Vote: How Voter Suppression Is Destroying Our Democracy*. Bloomsbury, 2018. 98.

2. Anderson, *One Person, No Vote*, 97.

3. Anderson, *One Person, No Vote*, 105.

4. Anderson, *One Person, No Vote*, 105.

5. Brian Klaas. "Gerrymandering Is the Biggest Obstacle to Genuine Democracy in the United States. So Why Is No One Protesting?" *Washington Post*, 10 Feb. 2017, washingtonpost.com. Accessed 1 Aug. 2019.

6. Thomas Wolf and Peter Miller. "How Gerrymandering Kept Democrats from Winning Even More Seats Tuesday." *Washington Post*, 8 Nov. 2018, washingtonpost.com. Accessed 1 Aug. 2019.

CHAPTER 9. THE TRUMP ERA

1. "Wide Gender Gap, Growing Educational Divide in Voters' Party Identification." *Pew Research Center*, 20 Mar. 2018, people-press.org. Accessed 1 Aug. 2019.

2. Jessica Taylor. "Republicans and Democrats Don't Agree, or Like Each Other—and It's Worse Than Ever." *NPR*, 5 Oct. 2017, npr.org. Accessed 1 Aug. 2019.

3. Carol Anderson. *One Person, No Vote: How Voter Suppression Is Destroying Our Democracy*. Bloomsbury, 2018. 129.

4. Andrew J. Yawn. "Felony Voting Rights Restored for Some in Alabama, but Many More 'Do Not Know They Can Vote.'" *Montgomery Advertiser*, 27 Mar. 2019, montgomeryadvertiser.com. Accessed 16 Sept. 2019.

5. Brian Naylor. "'Black Votes Matter': African-Americans Propel Jones to Alabama Win." *NPR*, 13 Dec. 2017, npr.org. Accessed 1 Aug. 2019.

6. Gregory Krieg. "Stacey Abrams Says 'Democracy Failed' Georgia as She Ends Bid for Governor." *CNN*, 17 Nov. 2018, cnn.com. Accessed 1 Aug. 2019.

7. Khushbu Shah. "'Textbook Voter Suppression': Georgia's Bitter Election a Battle Years in the Making." *Guardian*, 10 Nov. 2018, theguardian.com. Accessed 1 Aug. 2019.

8. Shah. "'Textbook Voter Suppression.'"

9. P. R. Lockhart. "Georgia, 2018's Most Prominent Voting Rights Battleground, Explained." *Vox*, 6 Nov. 2018, vox.com. Accessed 1 Aug. 2019.

10. Mark Niesse. "Georgia Certifies Election Results after Nearly Two Weeks of Drama." *AJC*, 17 Nov. 2018, ajc.com. Accessed 1 Aug. 2019.

11. Eli Stokoles. "Why Trump Says It's All 'Rigged.'" *Politico*, 2 Aug. 2016, politico.com. Accessed 1 Aug. 2019.

12. "Election Fraud Cases from Across the United States." *Heritage Foundation*, n.d., heritage.org. Accessed 1 Aug. 2019.

13. Eli Rosenberg. "Kris Kobach Used Flawed Research to Defend Trump's Voter Fraud Panel, Experts Say." *Washington Post*, 7 Aug. 2018, washingtonpost.com. Accessed 1 Aug. 2019.

14. "Analysis: Noncitizen Voting Is Vanishingly Rare." *Brennan Center for Justice*, 25 Jan. 2017, brennancenter.org. Accessed 1 Aug. 2019.

15. Amy Sherman. "Trump Tweets That 58,000 Noncitizens Voted in Texas. That Hasn't Been Proven." *PoliFact*, 28 Jan. 2019, politifact.com. Accessed 1 Aug. 2019.

16. "Will Puerto Rico's Population Stabilize?" *Puerto Rico Report*, 14 Nov. 2018, puertoricoreport.com. Accessed 1 Aug. 2019.

17. Cassa Niedringhaus. "Puerto Rico Governor, Government Officials Advocate for Voting Rights in Boulder Hearing." *Daily Camera*, 5 Oct. 2018, dailycamera.com. Accessed 1 Aug. 2019.

18. John Wagner. "White House Spokesman Twice Calls Puerto Rico 'That Country' in TV Interview." *Washington Post*, 2 Apr. 2019, washingtonpost.com. Accessed 1 Aug. 2019.

19. Daniella Silva. "Fact Check: Trump Cites Misleading Statistics in Alleging Texas Voter Fraud." *NBC News*, 27 Jan. 2019, nbcnews.com. Accessed 1 Aug. 2019.

20. Vann R. Newkirk II. "Voter Suppression Is Warping Democracy." *Atlantic*, 17 July 2018, theatlantic.com. Accessed 1 Aug. 2019.

INDEX

ABOUT THE AUTHORS

DUCHESS HARRIS, JD, PHD

Dr. Harris is a professor of American Studies at Macalester College and curator of the Duchess Harris Collection of ABDO books. She is also the coauthor of the titles in the collection, which features popular selections such as *Hidden Human Computers: The Black Women of NASA* and series including News Literacy and Being Female in America.

Before working with ABDO, Dr. Harris authored several other books on the topics of race, culture, and American history. She served as an associate editor for *Litigation News*, the American Bar Association Section of Litigation's quarterly flagship publication, and was the first editor in chief of *Law Raza*, an interactive online journal covering race and the law, published at William Mitchell College of Law. She has earned a PhD in American Studies from the University of Minnesota and a JD from William Mitchell College of Law.

TRACI D. JOHNSON

Traci D. Johnson is an accomplished writer whose work has been featured on NPR and in literary journals. She has received grants from the Sustainable Arts Foundation and the Illinois Arts Council. Additionally, Traci's work has been recognized by the MacDowell Colony and the Fine Arts Work Center. She has also worked in educational publishing for 15 years. Traci lives in the Chicago area with her husband and three children.